Top left: Darwin city looking toward Frances Bay. *Top right:* The escarpment, Kakadu National Park.
Bottom left: Florence Falls, Litchfield National Park. *Bottom right:* Boats moored in Sadgroves Creek, Frances Bay.

The old Police Station and Courthouse.    The Beaufort Hotel and Darwin Theatre.    Parliament House.

The Uniting Church in Smith Street.

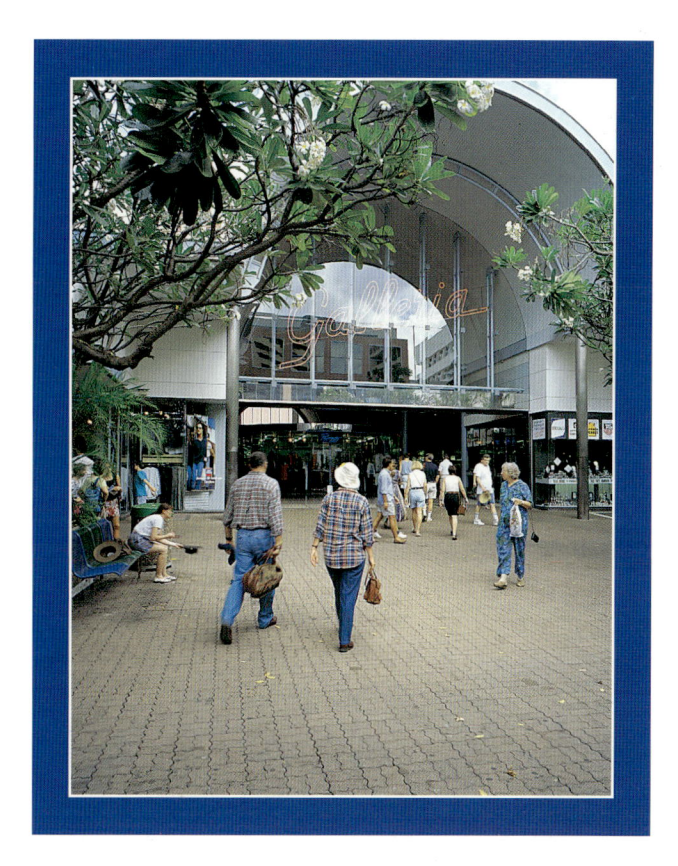

DARWIN, A TROPICAL CITY

Darwin, with its broad streets and exciting modern architecture, demonstrates the indomitable spirit of the Top End. Among the ultra-modern buildings are some from Darwin's earliest days that have survived wartime bombings and cyclones. The resilient citizens of Australia's most northerly capital are friendly and welcoming, making their city a favourite destination for overseas visitors and southerners (in Darwin terms, a southerner is anyone from anywhere else in Australia).

Well-served with first rate hotels and motels, Darwin acts as a focal point for tourists seeking access to its unique hinterland, but the city itself has much to offer. The shopping in Smith Street Mall is at least the equal of bigger cities in the south. There are beautiful beaches, verdant parks and gardens, and attractions such as world class restaurants serving food from around the world, the casino, cinemas, a symphony orchestra, theatres and museums.

Above: Smith Street Mall.
Opposite: Darwin, looking toward Frances Bay.

DARWIN DURING THE WAR

During World War II, Darwin was an important base for the Allied campaign in the Pacific. The city came under air attack, and 243 people were killed during the 64 air-raids. Today, the wartime gun emplacements are a reminder of this turbulent past and the East Point Military Museum has relics and information.

Left: A gun emplacement on the Esplanade.
Above: East Point Reserve with the Military Museum in the foreground and Fannie Bay in the background.

THE AVIATION HERITAGE CENTRE

The most impressive exhibit here is a B52 bomber on permanent loan from the United States. Other aircraft include a B25 Mitchell Bomber, Mirage and Sabre jets, a replica of a Spitfire, and the wreckage of a Zero fighter shot down in the raid on Darwin in 1942. Also on display are engines, armaments and a collection of photographs.

Above: Inside the Australian Aviation Heritage Centre.
Below: Fannie Bay.

The Variety Club annual "bash", Mindil Beach.

Bamboo sculptures on Mindil Beach.

Every Thursday, markets at Mindil Beach attract large crowds.

Imaginative and colourful floats at the Festival of Darwin.

Mindil Beach, where the annual Beer Can Regatta is held.

Aquascene, Doctors Gully, an open arm of the sea to which fish come to be fed at high tide.

Main photo: Vessels of the Darwin Sailing Club at anchor near Vesteys Beach.

An entrant in the Beer Can Regatta, Mindil Beach.

Crowds on the Esplanade during the Festival of Darwin.

Fishing, a popular Top End activity.

Sunset, that magic time of day.

A lone cyclist on Nightcliff Jetty.

The Diamond Beach Casino at Mindil Beach.

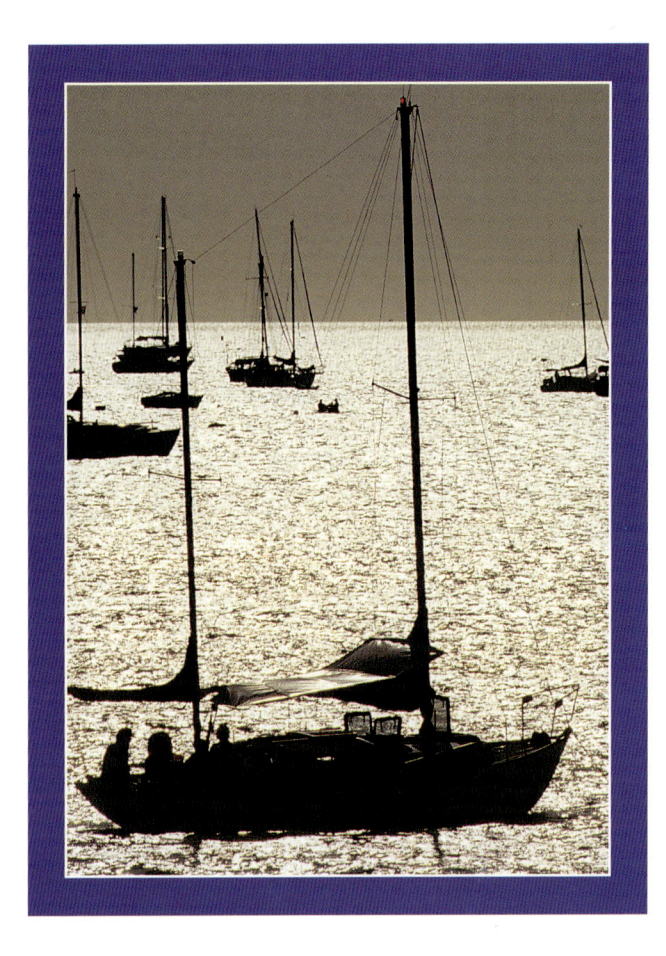

SUNSET – TECHNICOLOUR MAGIC EVERY DAY

Richly coloured sunsets are a daily miracle in Darwin. As brief as they are spectacular, they are best seen over the water, and people gather to marvel at the beauty of the colours and to relax as the cooling blanket of evening settles over the land.

Above: Yachts on the liquid gold of Fannie Bay waters.
Left: The glow of the embers of a glorious tropical day are reflected in the water and in the skies over Fannie Bay.

CROCODILES

Although saltwater crocodiles can grow to over six metres long and are capable of killing and eating adult humans, they do not constitute a danger to people taking reasonable precautions. They were hunted for their skin for many years, but now provide revenue for Top Enders mainly through the tourist trade. Tour operators treat salties with a great deal of respect for their power and intelligence, and for their survival skills.

Above: Reality versus fantasy – the smile on the saltie at left is at the prospect of food; the smiling, welcoming creature on the right attracts tourist for different purposes.

Even before Paul Hogan's popular Crocodile Dundee films, the crocodile was a recurring theme in the Top End. Crocodylus Park, near Berrimah, is a centre for education and research where visitors can observe crocs in their enclosures. The Gagudju Crocodile Hotel at Jabiru near the eastern boundary of Kakadu National Park (about 245 kilometres from Darwin by road), is built in the shape of a giant crocodile.

Right: An enclosure at Crocodylus Park.
Above Gagudju Crocodile Hotel, Jabiru.

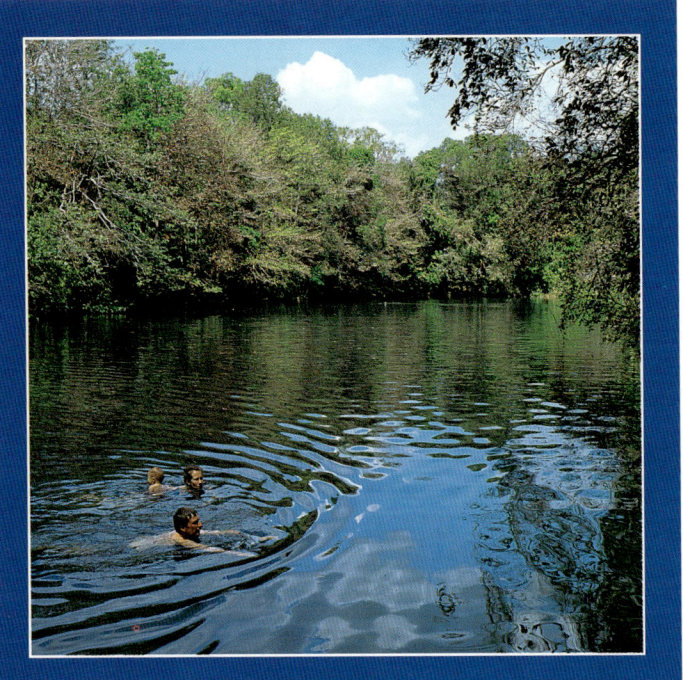

HOWARD SPRINGS

A short drive down the Track (Stuart Highway) brings lucky Darwin residents to the Howard Springs Nature Reserve, set in lush tropical rainforest. The sparkling spring waters are free of crocodiles, making this a popular swimming spot. As with all Top End waters, Howard Springs provide wonderful opportunities for birdwatchers and other nature lovers.

Above and left: Howard Springs.

Top left: A red-collared lorikeet. *Top right:* A female antilopine wallaroo.
Centre left: A northern snapping turtle. *Centre right:* A rough knob-tailed gecko.
Bottom left: A bush trail in the Territory Wildlife Park. *Bottom right:* A saltwater crocodile.

Above left: The road to Litchfield National Park. *Top right:* Imposing sandstone formations in the Lost City in Litchfield. *Centre right:* The entrance to the National Park. *Bottom right:* The town of Batchelor, "Gateway to Litchfield National Park".

LITCHFIELD NATIONAL PARK

An easy two hour drive from Darwin, Litchfield National Park is a pristine natural wonderland perched on the Tabletop Range, a huge sandstone formation renowned for its many waterfalls. Florence Wangi, Tolmer and Sandy Creek Falls are great attractions, with their crystal clear plunge pools fringed by lush rainforest. Huge termite mounds fascinate the visitor, as do the curiously eroded sandstone pillars known as the Lost City. Buley Rockhole is a very popular swimming and camping spot.

Top: "Magnetic" termite mounds.
Bottom left: People swimming in Buley Rockhole.
Bottom right: Tjaynera Falls.

Above: Wangi Falls, Litchfield National Park.

Above: Tolmer Falls, Litchfield National Park. *Following pages:* Florence Falls, Litchfield National Park.

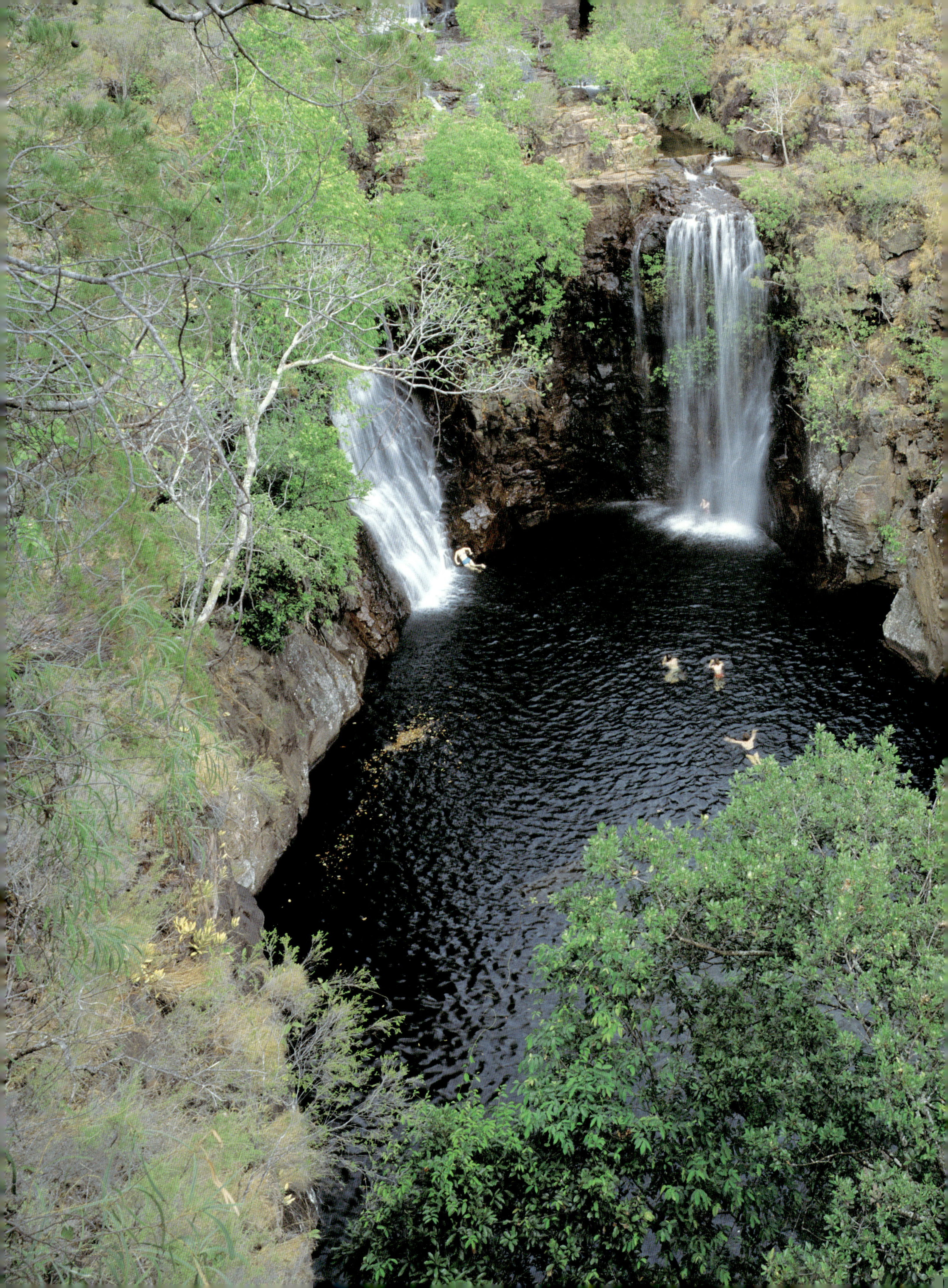

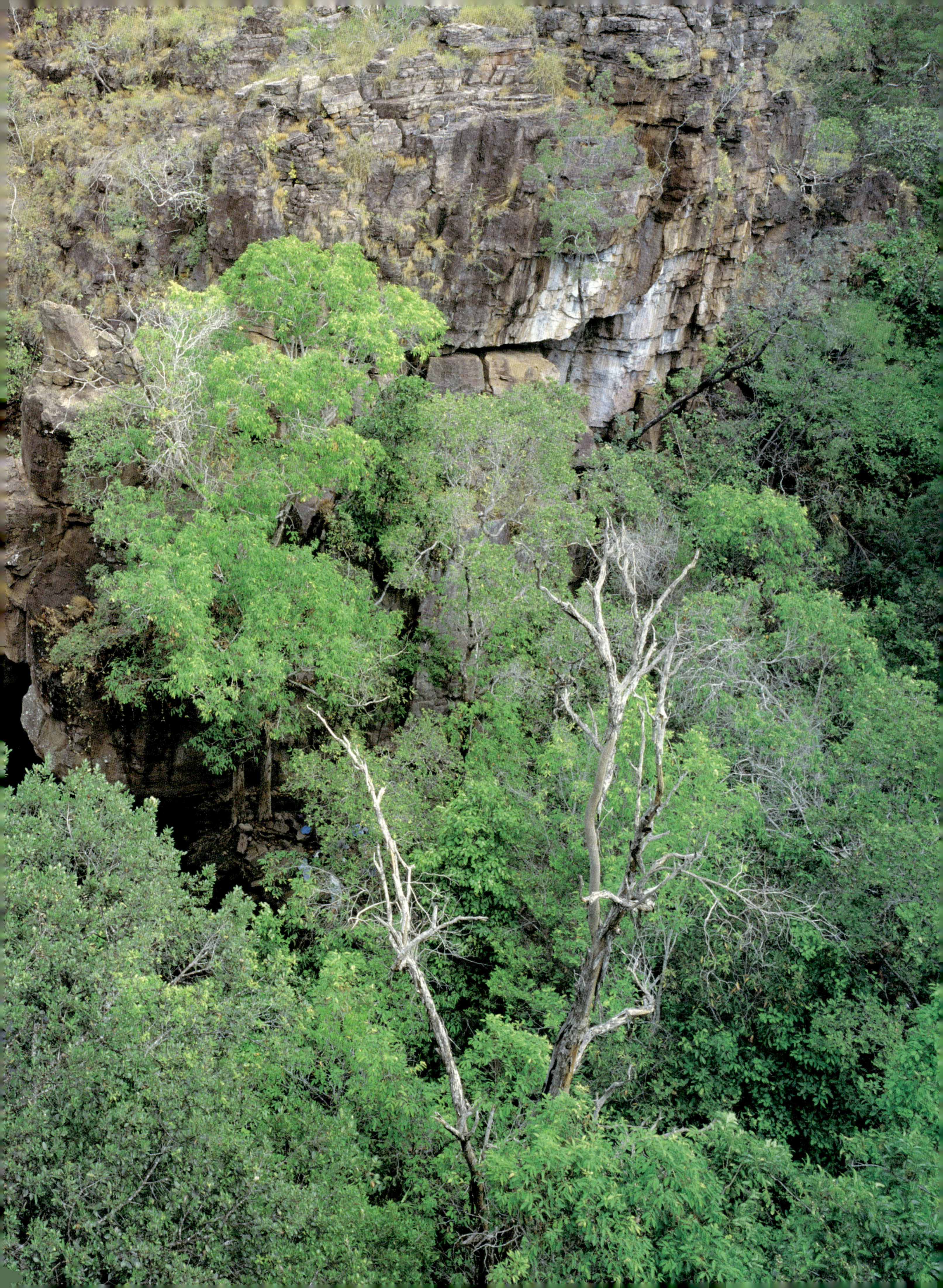

HIDDEN WONDERS OF LITCHFIELD

With corners of hidden delights in great variety, Litchfield offers an unrivalled richness of habitats; rocky outcrops, tropical rainforest, spectacular waterfalls and quiet creeks. The main attractions can be reached easily by sealed internal roads, and walking paths and camping areas make this natural wealth accessible to all.

Top and *bottom left:* Buley Rockhole.
Bottom right: Monsoon rainforest near Wangi Falls.

LAVISH LITCHFIELD

After the flat and rather bare country of the approach to Litchfield from the east, nature's lavish extravagance is revealed in the dense tropical vegetation of the park itself, where palms and vines reflected in the clear waters conjure up visions of a tropical Eden.

Top: Buley Rockhole.
Bottom left: Monsoon rainforest near Wangi Falls.
Bottom right: Greenant Creek.

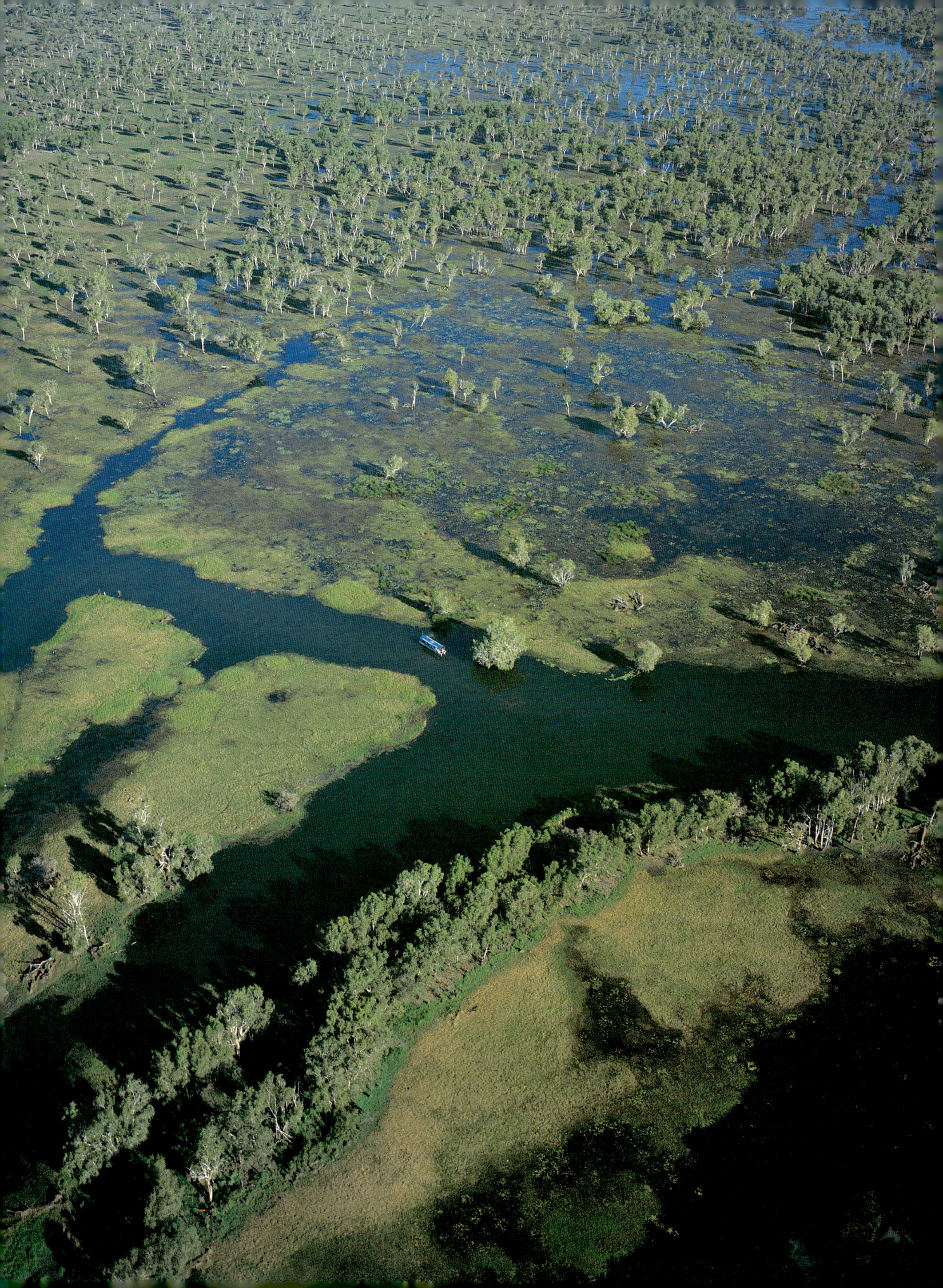

KAKADU NATIONAL PARK

The world-famous Kakadu National Park is almost 20 000 square kilometres of coastal mangroves, seasonal floodplains, paperbark swamps and tropical woodlands and forests, all overlooked by the towering sandstone escarpment that forms the edge of the ancient Arnhem Land Plateau. With such a range of habitats, this World Heritage listed marvel provides a uniquely staggering diversity of plant and animal life. The Aboriginal people who have learned its secrets over thousands of years are still its guardians.

Yellow Water, a vast wetland that drains into the South Alligator River, teems with waterbirds. Boat trips give visitors the opportunity to observe the wildlife and vegetation.

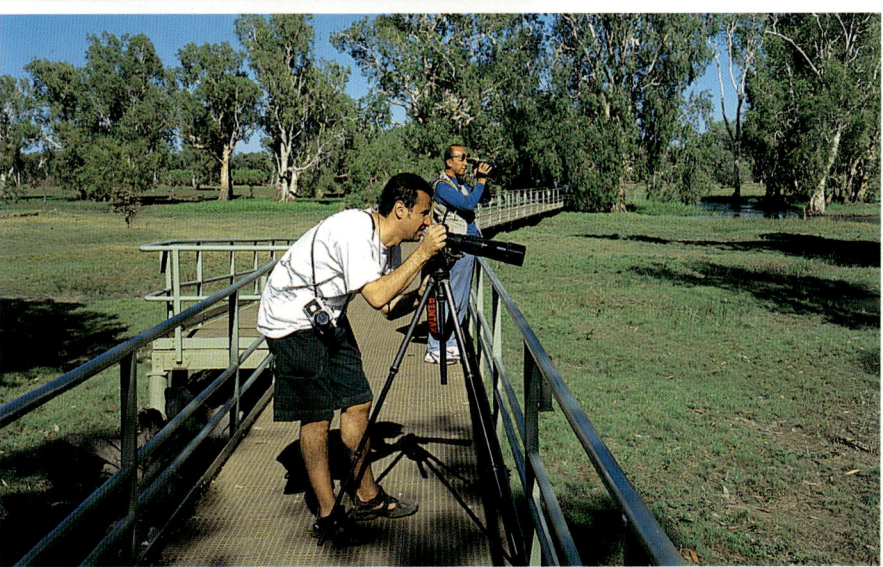

Opposite: Yellow Water, a vast expanse of wetlands. *Top left:* Cooinda and Yellow Water.
Centre left: A walkway at Yellow Water offers a vantage point for photographers. *Centre:* The wetlands teem with waterbirds.
Bottom left: Boating on Home Billabong near Cooinda. *Bottom right:* A saltwater crocodile.
Main photo, pages 30, 31: Reflections in the glassy surface of Yellow Water.
Main photo, pages 32, 33: A tourist boat on the wetlands.
Main photo, pages 34, 35: The majestic sandstone Kakadu escarpment.

Black-necked stork, or jabiru.

Flocks of waterbirds.

White-bellied sea-eagle.

Australian pelican.

Nankeen night heron.

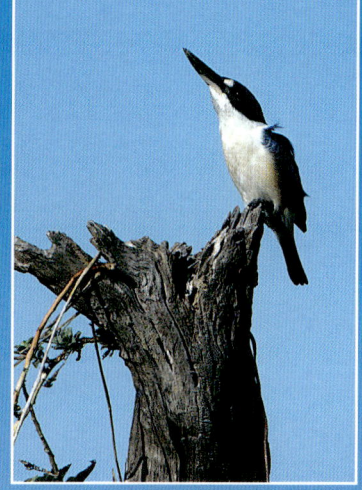

Australian darter.

A flock of waterbirds.

Forest kingfisher.

Comb-crested jacana.

Magpie geese.

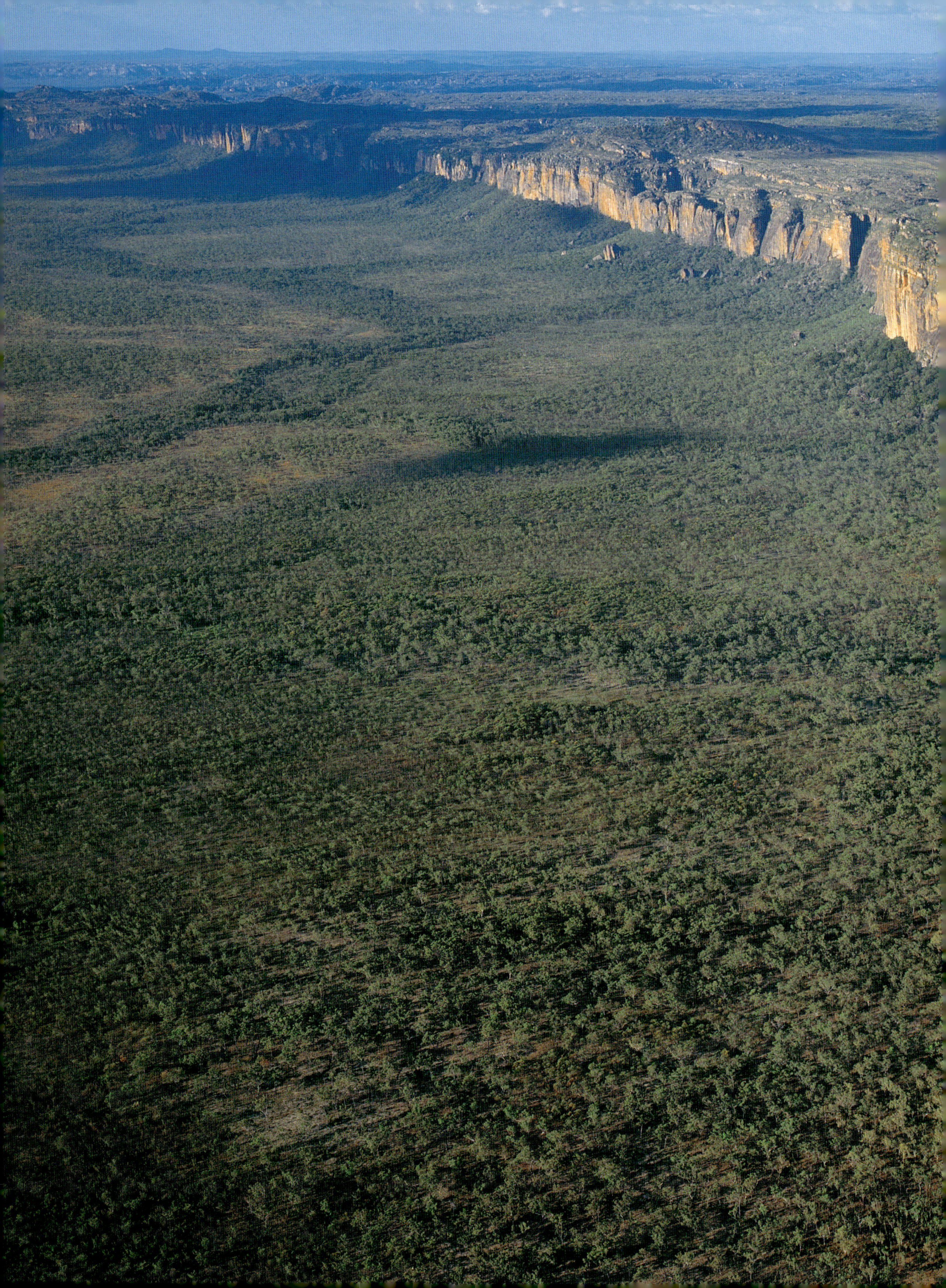

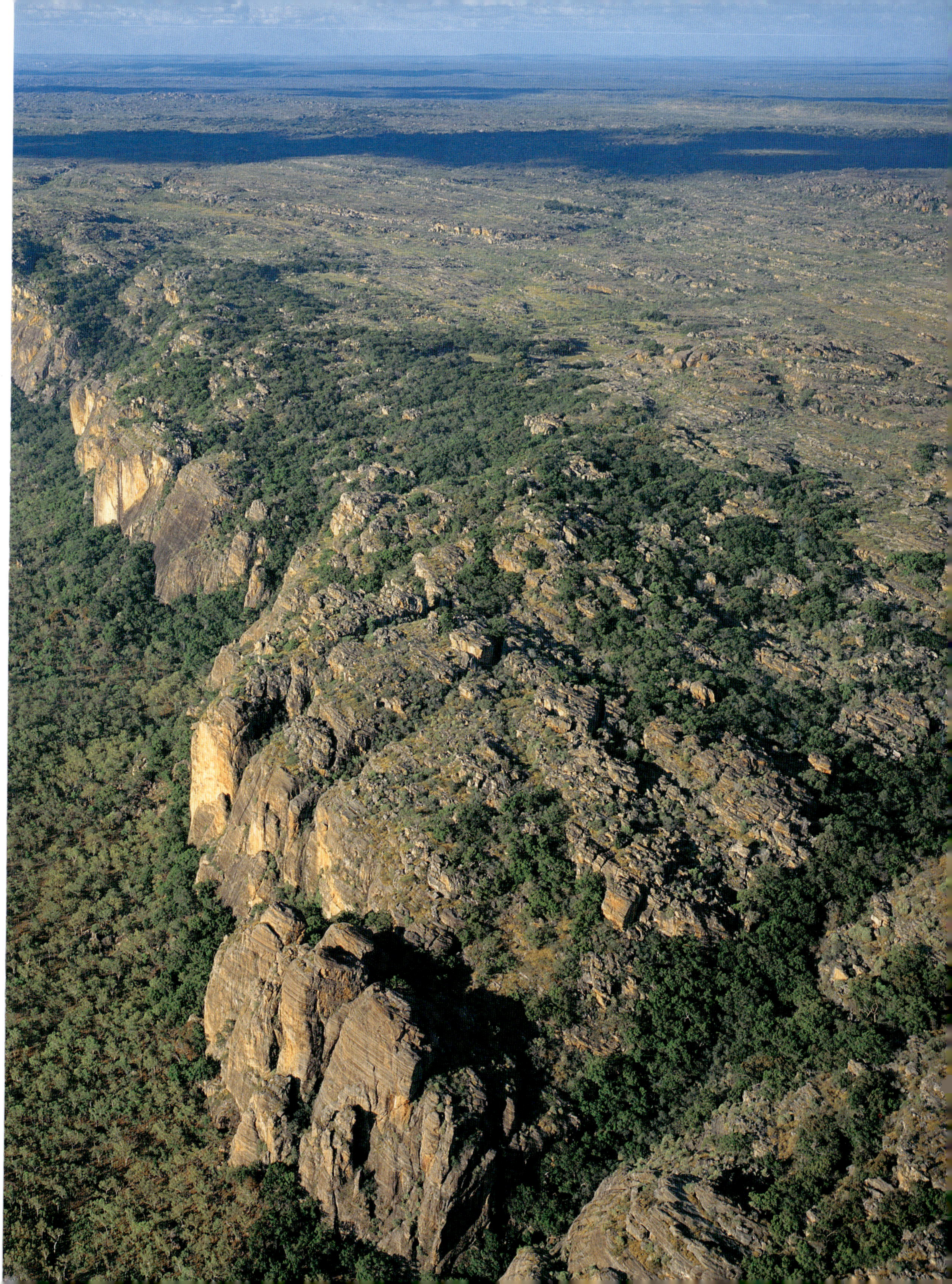

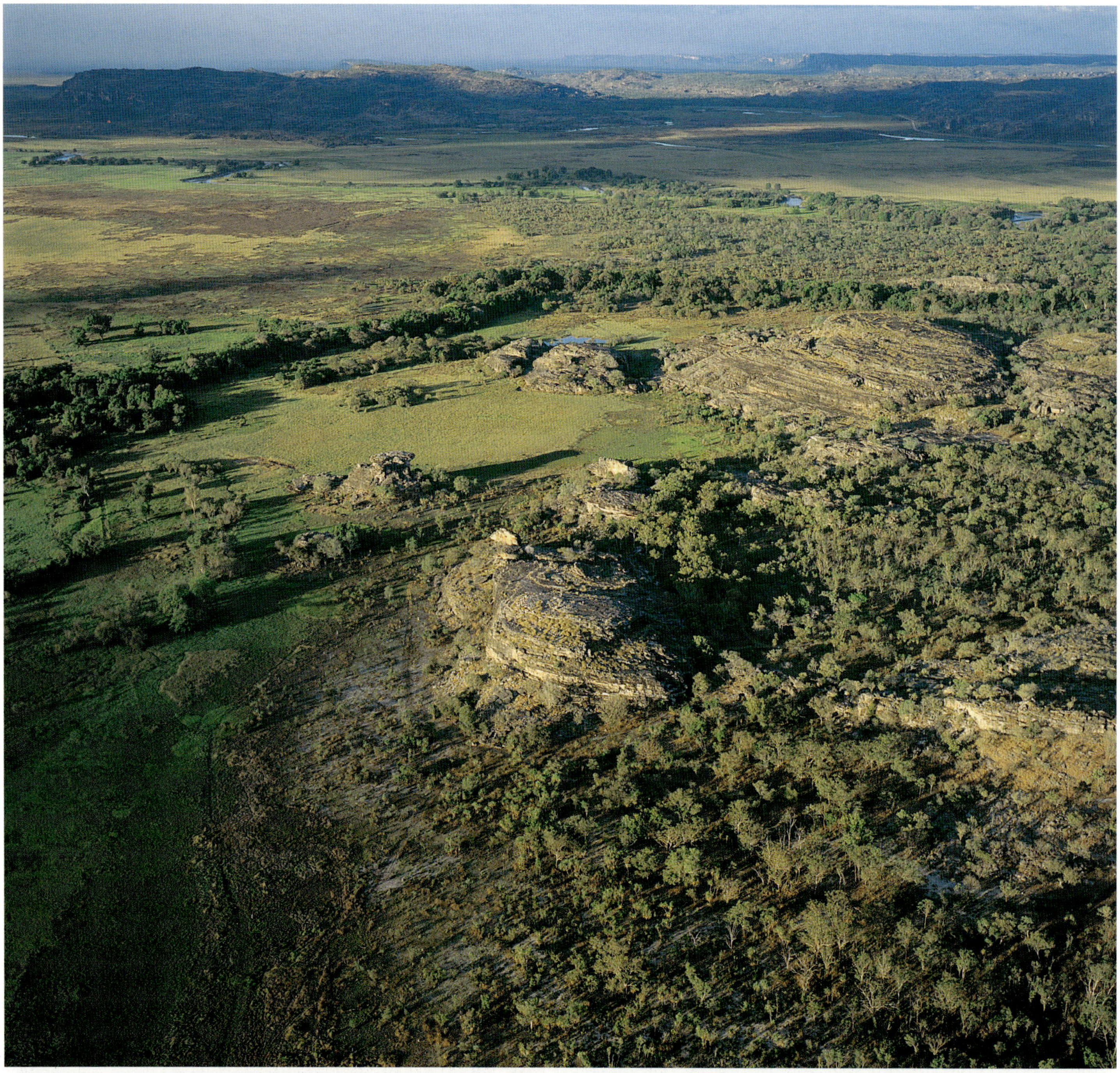

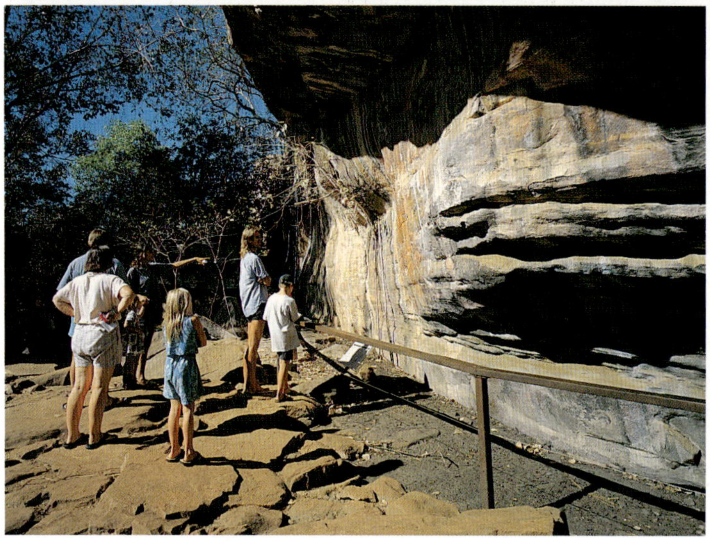

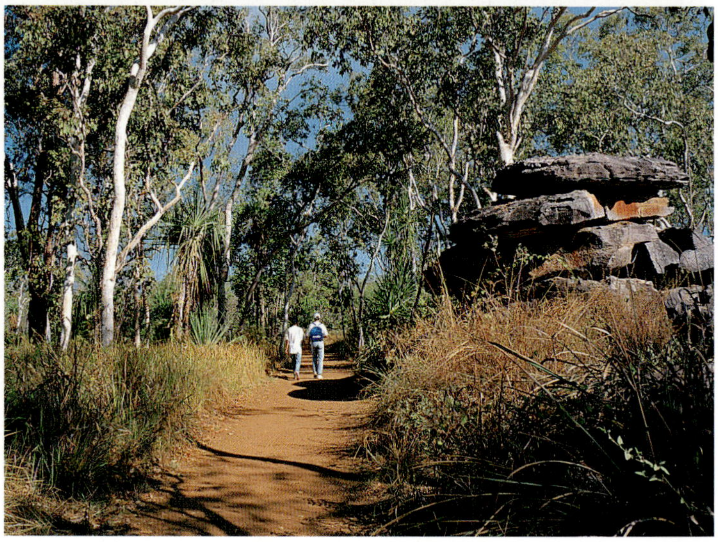

AMAZING UBIRR

Wonderful views of the wide floodplains of the East Alligator River await the visitor to Ubirr Lookout, a sandstone outlier. Nearby some of the most exciting Aboriginal art is easily accessible in several galleries, including the Main Gallery and Mabuyu Gallery. Some of the art could date back about 22 000 years or more, but most of it is of more recent origin.

Above: The panoramic view from Ubirr Lookout.
Opposite top: Ubirr stone country and floodplain.
Opposite bottom left: A fence protects the priceless art of Ubirr.
Opposite bottom right: A shady path to Ubirr's treasures.

ABORIGINAL CULTURE

The cycles of nature are central to the lives of the Aboriginal people of the Top End. The importance of the land and people's relationship to it are reflected in dance in the form of corroboree, with musical accompaniment from the haunting didgeridoo and beating of rhythm sticks. The dance tells a story, sometimes from the Dreaming, sometimes acting out a hunt or mimicking the actions of familiar creatures.

Left: Painted with ochre and clay, Aborigines prepare for a ceremony.
Above: Playing the didgeridoo and rhythm sticks.

WARRADJAN CULTURAL CENTRE

Built in the shape of Warradjan, the pig-nosed turtle, Warradjan Cultural Centre is in Cooinda Road at Yellow Water. The centre houses displays created by the Bininj people featuring important stories from their culture. Signs invite visitors to walk through the displays as a Rainbow Serpent moves through the country. As well, there are exhibits of art and artefacts, and a craft gallery.

Right and *below:* Visitors move through the displays of Aboriginal traditions, art and crafts at Warradjan Cultural Centre.

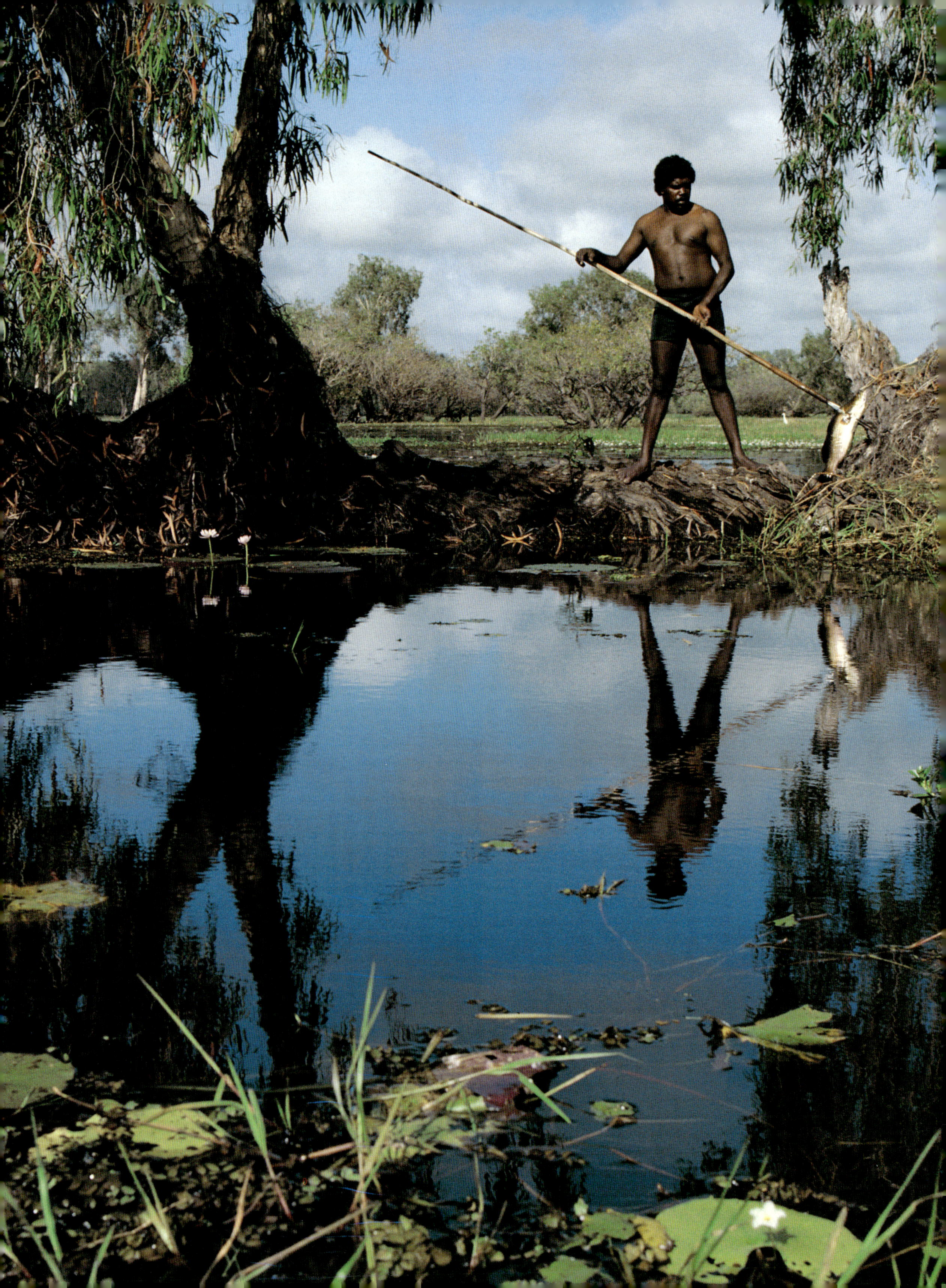

HUNTING AND GATHERING

Top End Aborigines enjoy a wide range of seasonal foods. Beside the hunting of birds and land animals, and the gathering of seeds, roots, berries and insects, there is a plentiful harvest to be had from sea and stream. For centuries Aborigines have made fish traps, and estuary and fresh waters have been fished with spears.

Above: Kapirigi gathers freshwater crocodile eggs.
Opposite: Jonathan Yarramarna lands a fish on a traditional barbed spear.

ABORIGINAL ART AND CRAFTS

Custodianship of the Kakadu area goes back tens of thousands of years. Throughout this time, the Gagudju people lived in harmony with this unique land and practised their traditional ways of life. Much sought after by collectors the world over, the traditional artworks and artefacts of Aborigines reflect their culture and utilise local materials that have been employed over the aeons.

Left: Gagudju people camp in the woodland. In the background, a bark painting is being created, and in the foreground are woven baskets. *Above:* Susan Aledjingu playing cat's cradle with friends. The shape created represents a turtle. *Opposite top:* Bluey Ilkirr, an artist of great skill, painting a marsupial on bark. *Opposite below:* Detail of an X-ray painting of echidnas hunting termites.

47

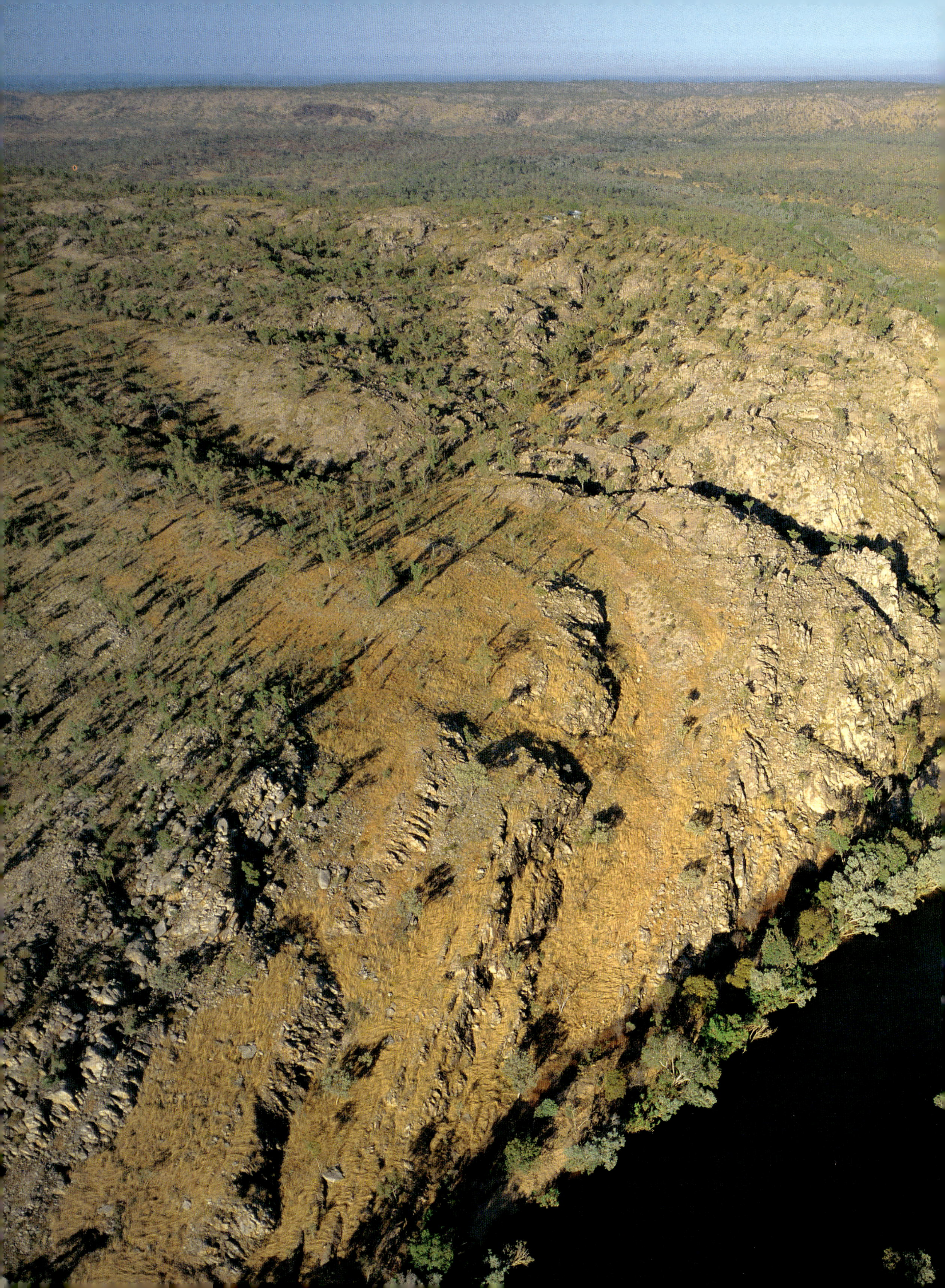

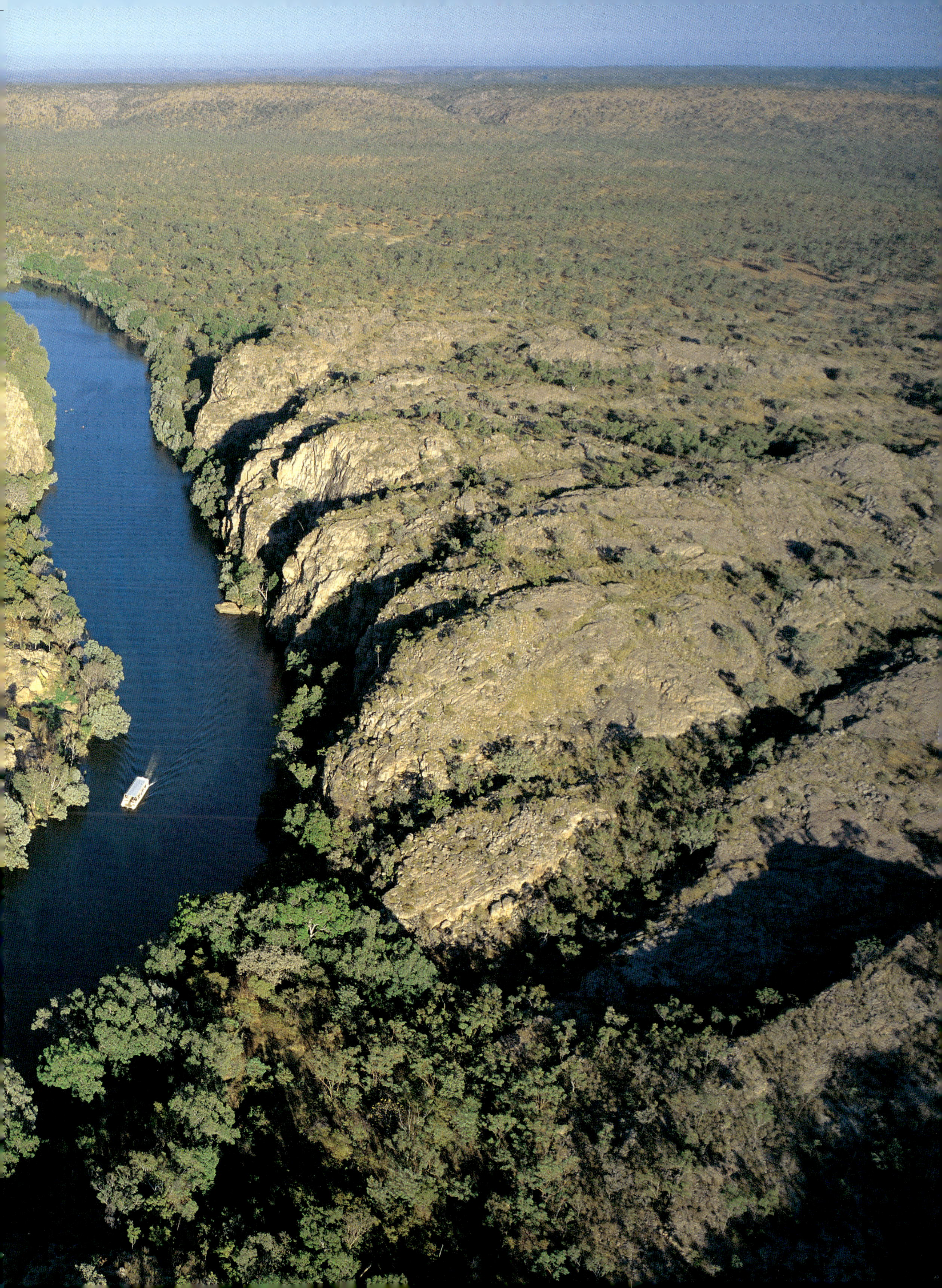

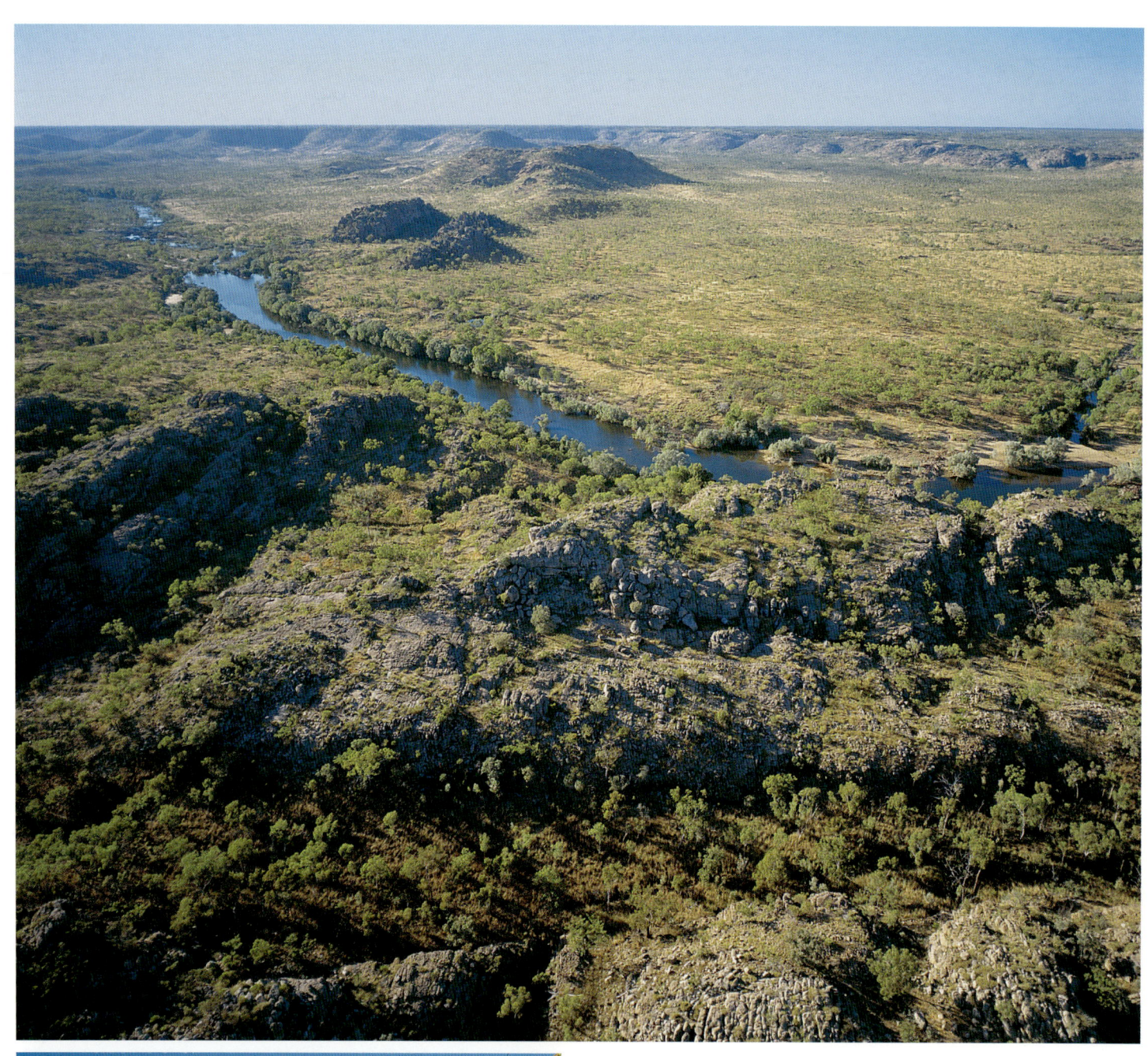

NITMILUK NATIONAL PARK

Some 300 kilometres south of Darwin on the Stuart Highway lies the large regional town of Katherine. Thirty kilometres east of the town, Nitmiluk (Katherine Gorge) is really a system of thirteen gorges carved through the wonderfully coloured sandstone over millions of years. Visitors may reach and explore the breathtaking beauty of Nitmiluk by road and air transport, boat tours or, for the really adventurous, there are canoes for hire. For bushwalkers, there are hundreds of kilometres of clearly marked tracks.

Above and *below* and *preceding pages:* Views of Nitmiluk, from the air and through the pandanus beside the Katherine River.

ELSEY NATIONAL PARK

Near to Mataranka, south of Katherine on the Stuart Highway, is Elsey National Park, which surrounds the homestead setting of Mrs Aeneas Gunn's famous pioneering story "We of the Never Never". Through the park runs the Roper River, with waterfalls and unexpected patches of cool rainforest. Here too is the remarkable Mataranka Thermal Pool, where a swim in the crystal clear water which is heated naturally to 34° Celsius is most invigorating.

Above: Feeding the fish from the banks of the Roper River.
Right: Mataranka Thermal Pool surrounded by rainforest.

52

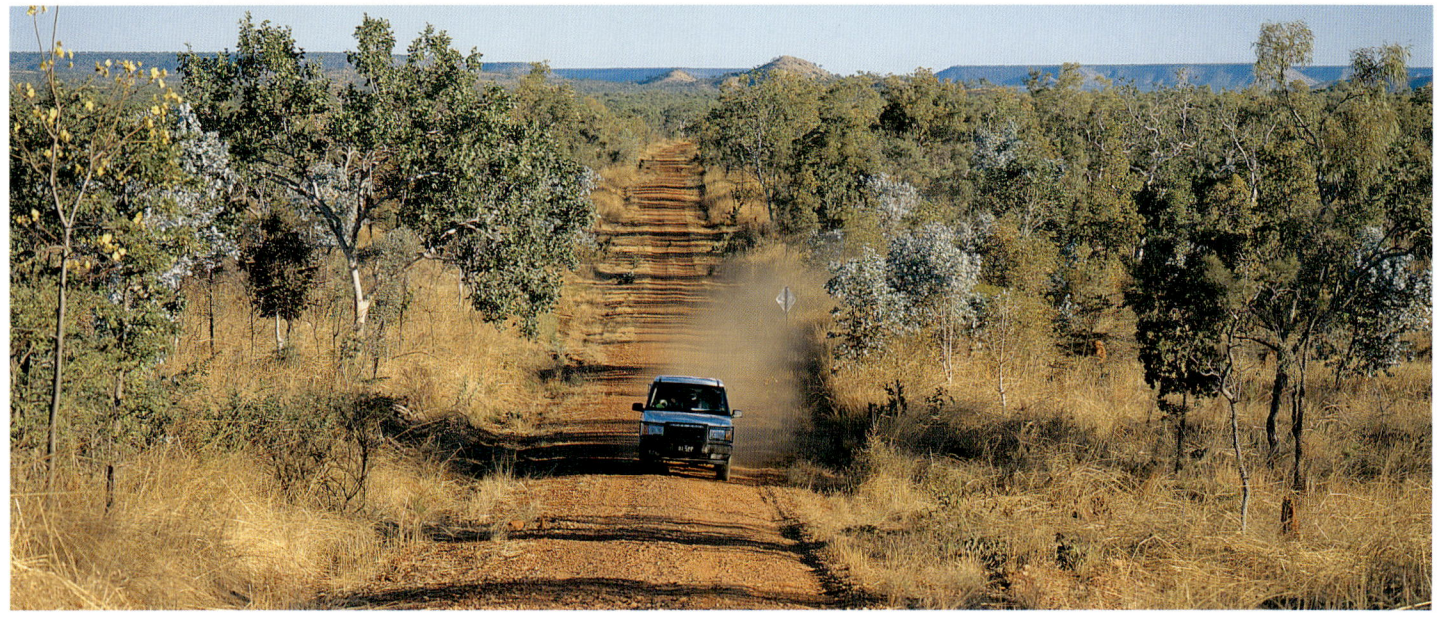

GREGORY NATIONAL PARK

Gregory National Park lies south of Timber Creek township on the Victoria Highway which links Katherine and Kununurra in Western Australia. It was named after the explorer Augustus Charles Gregory who carved the date July 2nd 1856 into the curious swollen trunk of a boab tree on the bank of the Victoria River. The broad streams in the huge park harbour saltwater crocodiles, but visitors taking reasonable care enjoy the fishing and boating safely. The park contains spectacular ranges, sandstone escarpment and dramatic river gorges, including the unusual Limestone and Jasper Gorges which are accessible by four-wheel drive vehicles.

Above left: A lone palm stretching high above the scrub. *Top right*: The wetlands of Gregory National Park feature lush vegetation and an abundance of wildlife. *Bottom right:* A long-tailed finch. *Opposite above:* Boab trees. *Opposite below:* Typical vegetation along the four-wheel drive road.

KEEP RIVER NATIONAL PARK

North of the Victoria Highway and almost on the border with Western Australia is this smaller but fascinating park, also displaying the curious boab trees with trunks so swollen that three men with outstretched arms cannot join hands around them. Stark escarpments and hidden gorges add to the grandeur and mystery. Caves and overhangs are rich in Aboriginal art, and the park supports a rich variety of wildlife.

Top left: A massive boab tree
Top right: Open forest is found in parts of the park.
Above and *left:* Large water-eroded caves contain Aboriginal rock art.
Opposite: The Keep River.

First published by Steve Parish Publishing Pty Ltd, 1997
PO Box 2160, Fortitude Valley BC, Queensland 4006, Australia

© copyright Steve Parish Publishing Pty Ltd, 1997

ISBN 1 875932 87 9

All rights reserved. No part of this publication may be reproduced, stored in a retrieval system, transmitted in any form or by any means, electronic, mechanical, photocopying, recording or otherwise without the prior permission in writing of the Publisher.

Printed in Australia

Photography: Steve Parish
   Photographic assistance: Phillip Hayson, SPP
   p. 12: Pat Slater
   pp. 14 (bottom), 15, 38 (left), 42, 44, 45, 46, 47: Belinda Wright
   p. 36: Stanley Breeden
Map supplied by MAPgraphics
Text: Neil Lovett
Design, editing, art and film production: SPP